CHINA

ANCIENT TIMES

Lori Dittmer

Creative Education · Creative Paperbacks

Published by Creative Education and Creative Paperbacks
P.O. Box 227, Mankato, Minnesota 56002
Creative Education and Creative Paperbacks are imprints of
The Creative Company
www.thecreativecompany.us

Design, production, and illustrations by Chelsey Luther
Art direction by Rita Marshall
Printed in China

Photographs by Alamy (Blue Jean Images, Peter Horree, LEJEANVRE Philippe, Photo 12), Dreasmtime (Keng62fa), FreeVectorMaps.com, Getty Images (byillustration, Dorling Kindersley, IMAGEMORE Co, Ltd., simon-long/Moment, Oleksandr Zheitobriukh), iStockphoto (jcrosemann, KY, seaskylab), SuperStock (Dorling Kindersley/Exactostock-4268)

Library of Congress Cataloging-in-Publication Data
Names: Dittmer, Lori, author.
Title: China / Lori Dittmer.
Series: Ancient times.
Includes index.
Summary: This cultural overview of ancient China situates the reader within the society, describing key aspects of daily life, beliefs, and architectural accomplishments such as the Great Wall.
Identifiers: LCCN 2018053202 / ISBN 978-1-64026-112-9 (hardcover) / ISBN 978-1-62832-675-8 (pbk) / ISBN 978-1-64000-230-2 (eBook)

Subjects: LCSH: China—Civilization—Juvenile literature.
Classification: LCC DS721.D57 2019 / DDC 931—dc23

First Edition HC 9 8 7 6 5 4 3 2 1
First Edition PBK 9 8 7 6 5 4 3 2 1

CONTENTS

05 Step into Ancient China

09 Daily Life

12 Afterlife and Ancestors

16 The End of the Empire

19 Inside the ... Great Wall of China

20 Ancient China Timeline

22 Glossary

23 Read More, Websites

24 Index

CHINA
QIN DYNASTY

Step into Ancient China

You tie your hair into a bun. Then you leave for a long day at school. Like other boys from **noble** families, you want to be an important part of the Chinese community.

The first people in China settled along rivers. Later, they formed **dynasties**. These family groups ruled the empire. The Xia dynasty was believed to be the first. It was so long ago that we do not know if this family was real or made-up.

Daily Life

The emperor led ancient China. Ruling power passed from father to son. Sometimes, another group took over the empire. A new dynasty began.

The nobles lived in comfort. Men worked in the government or military. Women worked in their home gardens. They also **embroidered** clothes. Only the wealthy wore silk clothing.

Early on, education was only for noble boys. Later, all boys went to school. Around 500 B.C., a teacher named Confucius came up with rules for living. Students learned these rules, too.

Most people in ancient China were peasants. Many were poor farmers. Their homes were one-room huts. Across much of China, people ate rice with every meal.

FIVE CONSTANTS OF CONFUCIUS

- **KINDNESS** — REN
- **JUSTICE** — YI
- **KNOWLEDGE** — ZHI
- **INTEGRITY** — XIN
- **PROPER CONDUCT** — LI

Afterlife and Ancestors

The people prepared for life after death. Emperors filled their tombs with items for the next life. Even peasants were buried with a few coins.

People believed that dead family members watched over them. Each home had a **shrine** to the family's **ancestors**. The Spring Festival is still an important Chinese holiday. It is also known as Chinese New Year.

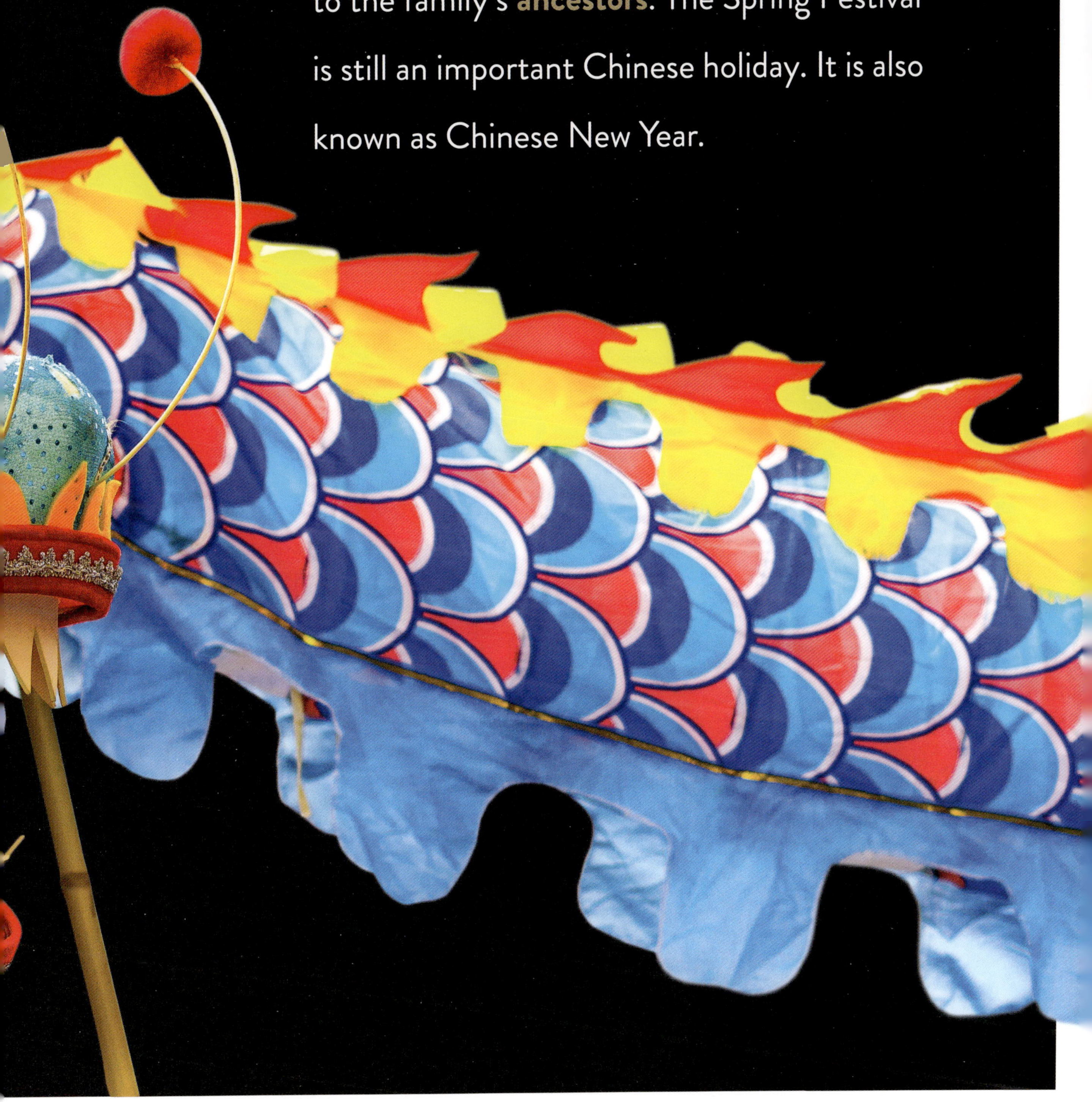

The End of the Empire

By 1840, 410 million people lived in China. They came from many different ways of life. This led to conflicts. In 1912, Sun Yat-sen became the country's president. The days of the dynasties were done.

INSIDE THE ...

Great Wall of China

Around 220 B.C., the Qin dynasty connected walls across northern China. Later dynasties added on to this wall. Today, the Great Wall spans more than 13,000 miles (20,921 km). Millions of people visit it each year.

CHINA TIMELINE

A.D. 618–907

The Tang dynasty becomes a "golden age" for poetry and the arts.

A.D. 105

Papermaking is invented during the Han dynasty.

1000s

The Song government is the first in the world to issue paper money for a nation.

2070 B.C.

As legend has it, the Xia dynasty begins.

c. 1600 B.C.

The Shang dynasty rules in the Yellow River valley. Shang objects are the earliest signs of Chinese dynasties.

220s B.C.

The Qin dynasty connects walls, forming the basis of the Great Wall.

551 B.C.

Famed teacher and thinker Confucius is born.

1572

At age 10, the Wanli Emperor starts his 48-year reign, the longest of the Ming dynasty.

1912

Sun Yat-sen becomes president of China.

Glossary

ancestors: people from whom one is descended

dynasties: lines of rulers from the same family or group

embroidered: decorated fabric by sewing patterns on it with thread

noble: of a higher class

shrine: a place of religious worship or remembrance

Read More

Morley, Jaqueline. *You Wouldn't Want to Work on the Great Wall of China!: Defenses You'd Rather Not Build*. New York: Franklin Watts, 2017.

Oachs, Emily Rose. *China*. Minneapolis: Bellwether Media, 2018.

Ponto, Joanna, and Fay Robinson. *Chinese New Year*. New York: Enslow, 2017.

Websites

Chinese New Year for Kids

https://www.china-family-adventure.com/chinese-new-year.html

Learn more about the history and traditions of Chinese New Year.

DK Find Out! Ancient China

https://www.dkfindout.com/us/history/ancient-china/

Read about the artwork and inventions created in ancient China.

Note: Every effort has been made to ensure that any websites listed above were active at the time of publication. However, because of the nature of the Internet, it is impossible to guarantee that these sites will remain active indefinitely or that their contents will not be altered.

Index

ancestors 15

clothing 9

Confucius 10, 21

dynasties 7, 9, 16, 19, 20, 21

education 5, 10

Great Wall 19, 21

holidays 15

homes 10, 15

nobles 5, 9, 10

peasants 10, 12

rulers 9, 12, 21

Sun Yat-sen 16, 21

tombs 12